A SWAN'S NECK

on the

BUTCHER'S BLOCK

Dr Jenni Fagan is an award-winning poet, novelist, screenwriter and Doctor of Philosophy; she is published in eight languages. After the publication of her debut novel, *The Panopticon*, Jenni was selected as one of Granta's Best Young British Novelists; she has been on various prize lists, including the Desmond Elliott Prize, James Tait Black, *Sunday Times* Short Story Prize and the BBC International Story Prize. *The Sunlight Pilgrims* saw her win Scottish Author of the Year at the *Herald* Culture Awards. Her third novel, *Luckenbooth*, was praised in *The New York Times Book Review*, which named her 'The Patron Saint of Literary Street Urchins'. In 2022 Polygon published *Hex* as well as her sixth poetry collection, *The Bone Library*, written during her time as Writer in Residence at the Dick Vet Bone Library. Her memoir, *Ootlin*, is published by Hutchinson Heinemann. To celebrate two hundred years of Macallan whisky, Fagan was commissioned to write two hundred poems, which were published in a collector's edition: *The Heart of the Spirit*.

JENNI FAGAN

A SWAN'S NECK

on the

BUTCHER'S BLOCK

Polygon

First published in paperback in Great Britain in 2024 by Polygon, an imprint of
Birlinn Ltd | West Newington House | 10 Newington Road | Edinburgh | EH9 1QS

9 8 7 6 5 4 3 2

www.polygonbooks.co.uk

Copyright © Jenni Fagan, 2024

The right of Jenni Fagan to be identified as the author of this work has been
asserted in accordance with the Copyright, Designs and Patents Act 1988.

All rights reserved. No part of this publication may be reproduced, stored, or
transmitted in any form, or by any means electronic, mechanical or photocopying,
recording or otherwise, without the express written permission of the publisher.

ISBN 978 1 84697 676 6
EBOOK ISBN 978 1 78885 680 5

British Library Cataloguing-in-Publication Data
A catalogue record for this book is available from the British Library.

The publisher acknowledges support from the National Lottery through
Creative Scotland towards the publication of this title.

Typeset in Verdigris MVB Pro Text by The Foundry, Edinburgh
Printed and bound in Great Britain by Ashford Press, Gosport

For Batshiva & Belle, who brought their claws

CONTENTS

My Heart	1
Peripatetic	2
Ootlin	3
There's a Problem in the Arts	4
Ninety Seconds to Midnight	6
Last Orders	8
Memorial	9
Fanged	12
Orpheus	13
Who Are You to Say What It Is	
To Be Living?	14
Urchin	16
Pact	18
Reclamation (or) My Shaman is	
Better Than Your Shaman	19
The Butcher	25
They Come For Me	27
Sign	29
Don't Read the Reports	30
Heroine	31
Orphan at the Table	32
Swan Song	34
Freak the Fuck Out for Christmas	35
Halo	37
Perdition	38
Swan	39

The Gift	40
Vengeful Saint	41
Rat	43
Civil Servant	46
Getting Rid of the Body	48
So Hurt by All of It, I Thought Death Might Be Nice	50
Fuck That	52
Queer Dating	53
Window	54
I Don't Think	57
On Another One of My Worst Years	60
No Permission Slip Required	61
Benediction	62
Spinster	63
They Found Something in My Blood	64
Winter Solstice	66
Do What You Do	68
Things Said by XY Chromosomes	69
Polonium-210	73
Pre-Nuptial	75
Wild Winter Hag	77
Instead of Goodbye	78
Busy	79
I Forgot About Love	80
Ossification	83
Badger	84
Abstract Art	85

Clean Bones	86
Fuck it	87
Mental Control Laboratory	88
Struggling	89
Home	91
I Miss You Knowing Me and	
Being Able to Hold You	92
Homicidal Motivations	95
In Another Country	96
The Boquet	97
Let's Bang on About the Moon	100
Luminary	101
Mortar	102
Before He Dies	103
The Taker	104
She Played the Trombone, You Know	105
Triffid	107
Dead at the Helm	109
Singing Nina Simone to the Echo	110
One Day	111
I've Made Houses Perfect	112
Hope	113
Thank You	114
Acknowledgements	117

MY HEART

She opened her mouth, and a butterfly flew out.
She opened her eye, a chrysalis!

Two bridges slept, not so far away.
A clack of sails. Sunken harbour, mud worms.

Whilst we are on the back step,
you and me. You and me!

Eating our sandwiches (cheddar) you are two,
I am thirty-five, every day we do this,

look down the valley, sat on decking that needs
stripped back and varnished but isn't,

we are like a couple of little old men
happiest to just sit here, knee by knee.

PERIPATETIC

The very many homes of others
where
I
had to go stay . . .

I learnt to move through
each
one
fast, faster, fastest,

So fast in the end I'd cross a front door only to
walk
straight
out the back

without looking at a single thing . . .
I
didn't
like locked doors, or feeling shut in.

OOTLIN

On publication day
my books sit in a warehouse
in the dark, very much alive,
deadly as they ever will be,
whilst I am in the doctors
with my hair falling out,
rashes that won't go,
skin coming away on my hands;
the roots of a tree
sprout out through my stomach
and pull the doctor down
to where I can whisper (again).
It's been twenty-five years . . .
of getting sicker and sicker and sicker,
so I am fucking here . . .
in his office;
out the way at least of fascists, for a second,
do something, just one fucking thing . . .
that isn't looking at 'care' or prior 'drugs' or 'assaults'
on my file, or the tattoos on my arms,
or the fatness of my arse,
do fucking something!

Rather than each year just watch me get closer to death.

THERE'S A PROBLEM IN THE ARTS

Abusers, firstly, filing in,
then the cliques,
the tall poppy cutters,
the eternal side-eye,
the kids whose mummies and daddies
made them feel they were
the very most special
those who spit on strangers' souls
to soothe their ego
say it's only me me me me me me me me me meeeeee eeeeeeee
eeeeeeemmmmememmee –
it's an industry
for cunts!
Where's the fucking poetry in it?
They just can't be adored
enough; hiding their posh qualifications
so they can act like they are authentic, or working class.
So much hating
on the purest talent;
when they see it,
they blink as hard as they can
for a long time:

pretend to all   they can't see it,
pretend to all   they can't hear it,
make little digs in public or suck up to absolute vile predators
knowingly, whilst pretending to be feminists,
throwing those who always had far less than them

in their actual life,
under all the buses,
then running them over repeatedly
whilst waving their collections over their heads;
they will do literally anything,
to think that they are – it.
There is a problem in the arts,
I've seen so many of our greatest writers be erased –
by all the above
it makes me think of Sandie Craigie,
she would have totally got this.

NINETY SECONDS TO MIDNIGHT

That's what we got on the doomsday clock . . . closer than it's ever been, what does it mean? what does it mean? Send the children into school where they fight fight fight because the adults are fucking insane and their planet is ninety seconds to midnight . . . scientists say it is set for collapse – ten seconds closer than it has ever been, what does it mean? What does it mean? Tell the children all the lullabies and lay them down to rest whilst psychopaths kill the planet and we all think we did our best and just sit back now whilst they do it until they turn to kill us all . . . it's a malevolent evil to leave the writing on the wall, I don't care for the Bulletin of Atomic Scientists, I don't care to know children and other humans are freezing to death, or dying in fright whilst the bombs and the soldiers go bang bang bang. Who let the world be run by psychopaths? This is just a home run like the Son of Sam where they get to kill kill kill for the sheer fuck of it . . . there is no other reason to destroy so many lives, than you exist on evil and anyone cut too pure with hatred and a total lack of empathy ... it should cancel them out for all major jobs . . . certainly running fucking countries and anything to do with being in charge of armies, or fucking bombs, it's ninety seconds to midnight and I do not sleep well – nightmares every night and another day knowing that hell is a human creation and it is fed by malignant people; it is fed by money; it is fed by greed; there is no doubt about it we humans are not even remotely created equal – those who hurt others in such a fucking psychotic way are so far beyond demented and from each and everyone one of them this planet and her people should be permanently protected . . . so put in a clause for all of humanity, do it now for fuck's sake – don't let psychopaths run countries or the legal systems or the state . . . don't settle for more

– 6 –

seconds on the doomsday clock – this is our world right now to save
and we truly cannot stop . . . because the children we are leaving need
us right fucking now . . . not tomorrow; to alter every trajectory
they should never have to inherit and all the injustices no life could
ever merit . . . and isn't it ironic that the scientists who designed
the Doomsday Clock also designed the Atomic fucking Bomb –
scientists, commissioned to do that, instead of stopping it, instead
of altering it, instead of globally refusing to do anything that might
murder even one more person, ever . . . for the rest ay humankind,
we have it in us to change – everything but psychopaths took over the
whole fucking show and they will destroy all of our lives cos there's a
dark energy in this universe with true evil at its core and it is resident
in the human story and we cannot take this any more – it's ninety
seconds to midnight, what is wrong, what is wrong, what is wrong,
with humanity, what is wrong? . . . that for all we have achieved we
have been told to settle – for this, blood-stained, song.

LAST ORDERS

I picked up the tab
for your entire fucking life . . .

I paid for yours – with mine,
I am still paying.

Still, you didn't understand
my reputation in the next world

Did ye, Dad?

Until now, just as you've arrived . . .
It's last orders at the bar unnaw, so good luck – wi aw that.

MEMORIAL

When you died
I had nothing to hold on to,

others had memories,
shared stories,

a place they could go
to bring your body back

to warmth,
while I got only

what you gave me,
which was nuhin

but pain & so
much worse; yer death

made me remember
how worthless

I was to you,
you tainted me.

In this memorial
of all the lives

you never attended . . .
mine was the first.

When I was tiny (three)
I used to sleep in a dark room

that felt like the whole world
had turned black

& I'd never get back
to the earth, or people,

a total sensory deprivation,
an isolation without light . . .

my name was taken,
like all I'd never get to be,

I was so far from safe,
just me & an unbearable ache,

cos nobody was coming,
not for me, not ever –

whatever I had to survive
it was on me; it's taken nearly

forty-six years
to be able to feel that particular

level of pain and loss again,
from that exact time,

I don't know how you died
fir sure, even the most basic

decency was never afforded
in my direction, not on birth,

or in the end, just jagged
hatred from other's fronds,

even more barbs to cut into my skin
I was never a daughter

not in death, not in life,
for your actions,

I have paid so, very, many, times.

FANGED

My mother stared at the moon
with her belly full of bones
and organs
and my bloody little beating heart,
and so I went mad . . .
a fanged thing –
so they say, so they say.

My mother was a light switch,
electrocuted on demand,
there was no money in the meter after that,
so she sent me to a lot of other mothers,
who saw the madness
of her in me,
just a little thing of hers, that I could carry.

ORPHEUS

It was only after his death that he became a swan,
she did not see him . . .
yet from her exceptional vantage point away up above the pond
(hiding from the others)
at night she sees Cygnus,
a constellation known as the Northern Cross,
she'd like to be gliding
across the water lit up as it is by night and stars,
yet the others, well, what do they know about asterism?
Or ethics, too, for that matter.

WHO ARE YOU TO SAY WHAT IT IS
TO BE LIVING?

Let me say that I have lived
on my final day
even when it was only possible at times
to do small things
like look out a window.

Let me say I have lived:
even if I spent too much of it
wondering about dying
or plucking up all my courage
just to leave the flat.

Let me say I have lived:
when terrified,
when panic stricken,
when feeling half mad with grief,
when crossing an unlit street.

Let me say I have lived;
light always too bright,
the roads like waves
but I still found a way
to paddle through anxiety.

To be honest
I was told quite cleanly
that living

was really absolutely
not for the likes of me.

Certainly nobody designed
it easy,
not at all; in fact,
it was fucking impossible
there were so many times,

countless,
that I'd break, and break,
but even
in my breaking,
do not be mistaken,

I was still alive,
let it be said, on all days,
even the very worst,
even the most lonely,
I lived, I lived, I lived!

URCHIN

What am I to say
of the sea in my house?

So many floating bowls;
a bright red plastic toy gun sinks.

What am I to say
of this sea?

I get out of bed in the dark.
Listen, it watermarks the stair ...

Saltwater riddles loose sullen nails.
There is a striped sofa; I never liked it.

Lightbulb reflects fishes
swimming into a guitar cavity –

the very last gift my dead love bought me.
No, I don't play it.

A great evil slapping of water.
The warble of gone ...

If only the sea will claim me.
It's the sea I will not leave.

It pushes sand along shores,
tiny granules of whooshing glass

smooth the memories of centuries,
I won't tell on the sea.

It's tired. I know why it found me.
Only the sea can cradle an urchin.

Only the sea, only the sea!

PACT

Whenever I'm travelling
I still look for you.

We all agreed you were gone.
Honestly, everybody said it.

But you and I know
that it's not actually true.

Neither of us will ever die,
not as long as the other one is still alive.

RECLAMATION (OR) MY SHAMAN IS BETTER THAN YOUR SHAMAN

It was a time of reclamation;
I drove to see the shaman,

past a police station
where I had been held as a child,

beyond the green gate
and the church whose outdoor tree lights

lit up the kids' home I was in
(almost on my own) that Christmas,

up a farm lane
where I'd stayed as a runaway kid

with a young (ish) guy
who I'd met in the village one time,

onto where green views flattened,
so it looked to me like Oregon;

cattle grazing and that gentle blue
of a sky kissed by summer's

hope and everything I remember
of driving across America:

always writing, writing . . .
turning into a drive

where a dog barked –
ferocious (so wee and lovely really)

down through a garden
where a carved wooden totem ages,

duck under a small door,
a stone-built room: tiny, one window,

sit cross-legged on the floor,
the shaman and I at first,

and then, too, there are
her guides appearing here,

and a wolf that I call to me,
my future self too, who has come

from thirty years ahead,
in her life by the sea . . .

The shaman drums
her ancestors into the space,

mine too, until we are all of us
ready, to go back to a room

where an infant warrior
had laid alone,

for far too long; I want to
carry her out of there on my hips,

bring her up through all levels,
so she will never

lie in the dark again.
It is the night before

my forty-sixth year; it's taken
me every day until now

to be ready to call back
the parts of my soul

who wandered furthest,
the parts who fought the most

with the least, who were
out there in limbo

for the longest of times,
just waiting, to one day

hear drums in the distance,
a call of the wind,

the wild steady heart of the sea,
there are so many night skies

to pass under, to get to this child,
can she feel we are on the way?

Walking across starlit fields,
I am still so sick from a descent

I started months ago, to begin
this exact journey to here;

my wolf keeps me steady,
they know my future self, see,

& we journey in silence,
for a faerie child,

who is stronger
than all of us,

so much in her to admire,
fought with less than nothing,

still, refused to let go,
yet it is only ... this year,

where she decided
it was time, finally,

to open the door ...
and find all of us,

walking towards her ...
down a bare hall,

all these rooms
are now empty,

she has waited so long ...
this is the work

of soul retrieval;
I missed this child.

I did not want to leave her
like this, but we were separated

by lightning that should
have been the end of us both

yet, here, forty-three years later,
I extend my hand to hold;

together we are one for the first time,
taking a step towards home.

THE BUTCHER

Likes to sharpen his knives
whilst listening to two-tone tunes up loud.

He is paler than plucked chicken,
he has the sinews of a serial killer.

He has real promise! Could be one of the greats!
A physique designed to slab the fucking steak.

Just so, just so, he does it just so,
just so, just so, machete cleanly cleaves gristle, just so!

He says he'll love me. Don't they say such things!
How will he do it? How?

It's a question I never used to dare ask,
so starved as I was for scraps, now I dare not ask,

I dare not! Have to ask it. He is onto the fillets.
He likes to sharpen, sharp, sharpen his knives

I lay out the long swan of my body,
wings ruffle, shoulder blades sharper than a human's.

I could break a leg with little effort.
He knows it, he knows it . . .

turns the radio up,
looks into the clear red blood of my eyes.

THEY COME FOR ME

Night pours through my bedroom door –
the endlessness of shadow life –
spiders furred and long-legged and precise
seek ears in which to drool chelicerae;
quiet blinking eyes, Tasmanian devils in the forest mind,
the squat rat, half-bat,
a round gold moon-sounding his gong without sympathy,
the webbed dreams,
the frozen sleep,
the ancient darkness;
all of the dreamers torn by absent suns,
by the astronomical vast . . .
by how every twilight concedes to a deep umbra,
to no gegenschein,
to the dead stars,
to all the cold alleys strewn with litter,
to all the alone people thinking
of all the other alone people that they will never meet . . .
each of them never more acutely divided
than at the witching hour:
to those scared of all of being . . .
they come for me, those nights!
They do.
They find me out on a dirt track,
a pack of wild dogs walking behind me in silence,
I don't try to go home anymore,
I don't trust houses, or doors, or beds, or sleep, and when they say
I'm so very brave – like I chose all the monsters & melted them

– 27 –

down

into shallow silver soup spoons . . .

I hand out those tarnished implements to a group of wild children,

so they may drum on the roofs of idiots –

louder, and louder,

like metal rain.

SIGN

Send me a sign
that you loved me,
in life,
just a tiny one will do ...
anything, like the memory of how you would wiggle your ears
to freak me out when we were too high,
too young, so beautiful,
or how I once told you to knock my door
after you'd been at some mad rave,
but only if the light was on,
how I took a piece of paper and drew a huge bright lightbulb
and placed it in my window,
lest you miss,
that I was still waiting for you even in the darkest hours of night.

For you, my light was always on.

DON'T READ THE REPORTS

I get up,
clean the flat,
find a way to leave my mind;

I don't go to Saint-Tropez,
I don't get a tan,
I don't believe the hype;

I am not thin,
I also look like shit,
I don't care, I just type;

look, see, survive,
I choose a Livienne sofa,
over love's acrid sigh;

I always leave –
go off to create
worlds in which others

will hang out awhile;
know this chia,
I am still so fucking alive!

HEROINE

You always did smoke like a true cancer seeker.
180 oxy per month is like more than six a day, no?
We as a family love opiates.
I'm not buying.
I'm not ever sleeping again either.
I'll stay wide awake now and always watching.
When it came to gobble you up . . .
you hit it twice as hard, ay?

A Benedictine prayer of madness . . .
left me with another fucking lifetime of sadness.

ORPHAN AT THE TABLE

There's an orphan at the table
acting like a daughter,
there's an orphan at the table
no-one will say who brought her,
there's an orphan at the table
defying social order . . .
there's an orphan at the table
she's got a tongue like a slaughter
there's an orphan at the table
barefoot with an empty bowl,
there's an orphan at the table
voice of the sea, eyes so gold,
there's an orphan at the table
lost more than any could take,
the overkept won't look at her
for fear of what they will see
they eat her honour in silence . . .
whilst she sits in hunger and bleeds,
I love her, this precious girl,
take my shoes off for her, sing to
her the blues, give her water,
warmth, food, she is every god's
most beloved child, she has more
to teach than most, of this life,
there's an orphan at the table
woven from the atoms of stars,
in each hand she holds a galaxy . . .
whilst all they see are her scars

she's the hope of every future
gift her safety and to be seen
make her welcome at every table,
to not feel belonging – for her,
is just a dream.

SWAN SONG

It was the Greeks
that first told a tale about her last song,
the only one,
she would ever sing in fact,
every semiquaver – a constellation . . .
it's said she never sounded more beautiful
than on that last, smooth note.

FREAK THE FUCK OUT FOR CHRISTMAS

I could not speak for ten days after Christmas;
didn't watch tv,
barely phoned a person.
It was the language of grief and her insane fucking tears –
three hail Mary's for my forty-sixth year,
cross yourself backwards.
I had to consider leaving
for good before I could choose to be here:
incomplete, imperfect;
I placed two moons in my eyes,
I met Order in a cafe and tore up her itinerary.
For every fracture I held,
I poured gold in the cracks;
each time I fell,
I fell all the fucking way –
no parachute, thanks, if these are my depths
I'll free-dive beyond all markers,
pass the point of breath,
I always did my descents solo,
I don't have the good car or any of that;
the exhaust fell off mine this morning
I still drove it through the city;
there is no husband,
or any kind of pear tree;
I don't know what your garden has to say about it,
my wife would not be so resentful,
not like yours . . .
I don't have a fucking pension, or life insurance, no inheritance

(just addiction – mental illness & extra lashings of trauma,
thanks so much, thanks, really, truly, thanks),
I never learned tae ski,
I hate all the ways people triumph over stuff that costs money.
So – you spent a lot of trees? Well done, ay.
Cunts!

HALO

I've had the kind of relationships that kill,
and those that revive the dead;
it wasn't always certain which kind I was having . . .

I denied myself a victim,
to everyone, to myself, to the three little pigs,
to that purple-bearded stoner troll under the bridge . . .

I said it wasn't abuse – even whilst it was all they fucking did;
swore on all bibles I was autonomy incarnate,
at three years-old, thirteen, twelve, twenty-two, thirty-nine,

besotted with fury, I learnt to transcend rage,
I knew – every relationship ended on the day I was born
every conception is a mechanical clock:

tick, tock, tick, tock.
I did the germinal stage, I was embryonic,
and suicide was in me, like it was in those before me . . .

first time I was ten inches long!
Just after the quickening,
she must have felt that flutter and sought to put it out:

like a cigarette, one of many . . . it's true
some people smoke relationships until they are burnt down
to the hot fragile end, falling ash, once again.

PERDITION

You agreed to go
to your eternal damnation
rather than look me in the face,

or my child . . .

guess it was easier
than knowing what you did,
exists in every breath

I will ever take.

SWAN

The swan has water retention;
thin people tell her she must radically accept being fat.
She is remembering when she worked in Wendy's burger bar –
some kind of McDonald's type thing –
she can't walk well lately,
so she carries a stick and her wide yellow feet flap in pain but still
she keeps going,
nobody calls her name,
she never was a Trumpeter swan,
no bugle calls from her to be heard from miles away (so fucking
uncouth)
help is never something;
it is not like she is a mute swan,
(those have twenty-three vertebrae more than all other birds)
her shoulders are winged,
each one hurts, budding as it does for flight;
on eBay she scans for a typewriter,
it has to have keys big enough to jab at with her wings,
as a female she is called a Pen,
which is funny, to her, as she picks it up, to start writing.

THE GIFT

They tried so hard to pass
their gargantuan grey and vast nothing onto you:
couldn't carry it
couldn't look at it
couldn't see it
couldn't hold it
couldn't give a fuck about
bequeathing it to you;
so mind blind,
so emotionally dead,
cutlery tray rattles long silver teeth,
tiny frogs bounce
across the kitchen floor
whilst everyone is asleep;
it's such foolishness,
to keep a witch's things,
still – when they took this, then that,
all the things that were not theirs to own,
pointed it all out – want this, want this one, that one, that too,
whilst they took and they took and they took,
you – quietly kept your sanity,
returned all emotional voids to their owners,
did not forward your address.

VENGEFUL SAINT

The wind chaps on all doors,
at 1.33 p.m.,
rattles letter boxes
on every street at once;

like any good
mafia shakedown,
it lets all sleepers know
it's this easy to find them.

At 2.57 a.m. foxes
slink along ivy walls,
a red-furred, sharp-clawed
pack of angels,

they are ever-alert
against dogs,
those idiot dancers.
I look into empty spaces.

At 5.47 a.m.
hope is
the darkest
fairy tale told.

Metal strikes the anvil,
a death clang,

we too shall soon
be gone.

At 6.01 a.m. I call
for my girl child,
she's sat in a corner
for four decades

waiting for me
to finally
learn her ways,
far too brilliant

is the light of her pain;
at 6.02 a.m.
I cancel the world.
It's outrageous.

All the vengeful saints!
All the vengeful saints!

RAT

I hear it scrabble, thirty-three minutes after midnight,
it is clawing through plasterboard,
chewing wood,
it wants, in, in, in.

I am up, light on just in time to see
a rat, big as my fist,
long tail,
scrabbling under the door

right into my bedroom;
it flies behind the wardrobe where I throw after it pure cinnamon,
it races back out, bolts up the side,
thick black tail hanging down.

Baseball bat in hand,
I trap it in the hall
then shut every other exit
coax it out of the pantry, out the front door.

The next day my neighbour –
turns into a rat,
a tall one,
wearing expensive trainers.

Guests arrive fir yuletide
whilst I'm cooking
I turn to find

a rat at my table drinking wine . . .

it watches me work
myself ragged with a smile
'Vermin, are everywhere
lately,' it says.

I know. I do know.
I know the rats.
I know how they take their loans.
Never pay debts back.

There's a rat
got my art and my furniture
to line his nest,
whilst to me he only detests.

Those cannibalistic
cosmopolitans!
A rat knocking at ma door,
A rat giving – Don't interrupt me, bitch . . .

I'll put you in your place!
A rat being a rat
in front of the only one I value,
eftir I made it lunch.

A rat, is a rat, is a rat,

a rat insisting he is not a rat,
rats do that,
a lot, rats working in offices . . .

rats on social media,
rats at the bank,
rats eating doughnuts in the hipster bakery,
rats avoiding the cat café . . .

Rats in denial, rats who don't
even know they are rats,
or they do,
but deny it.

A rat saying
I am a serious issue.
A rat insisting
that I am most mistaken.

Rat-rat, ratty rattiest
Of ratty rat rats,
Rat right off, rat, rat, rat,
Rat, rat, rat, rat, rat, rat, rat, rat.

CIVIL SERVANT

Has my kid's wooden drawers that cost me a ton,
won't give me them back because their sense of entitlement to my
        things was beyond insane.

I had ordered them from a craftsman ten years before,
hand crafted by plank, took six weeks to make, then two to get to
        Edinburgh,
and they were the first bit of decent furniture I ever bought;
at the grand age of thirty-five I finally got one expensive thing,
I thought it an investment to pass down to my child and maybe their
        kids –
it would in fact be the very first family heirloom;
seeing as I will inherit nothing but a fucking endless nightmare,
I was so proud of myself to get them, as a symbol that I was creating
        something solid
for my family, from far less than nothing:
an achievement, my two fingers towards no more abusive relationships.

Ten years later this civil servant turned up and threw a tantrum to take
        those drawers,
almost a decade after I had bought them, after I'd moved them through
at least eight houses that I'd totally killed my health to renovate, this
        civil, civil, civil – servant
wanted them why? To sell on eBay when I'm dead?

My things were never mine to him. Not my tears. Not my talent.

Not my kid's drawers,
especially not, my clear sight, and god forbid, the sanity of my
mind.

GETTING RID OF THE BODY

I thought it was him on the phone.
I thought after sixteen years he'd be at the door.
He'd meet my son.
I thought it would be far more awkward than fucking but
we might go for dinner.
We only ever met in bars.
Apart from one time
he drove me around big high rises in Glasgow
to show me where we came from
where he had once met the silhouette of my mother,
everyone was pretty chuffed to move in there,
they were a step up from slums.
They all had indoor toilets.
I wonder if we met six times?
I thought about how he'd talk about shagging my mother.
Open up a conversation on sex,
like a stain across clean white linen tablecloths
although railway tables are usually just formica.
His body, belongings, name, soul, are gone in days.
There is no question that I exist.
I don't.
I never did.
I offered to fly,
I offered to fly,
I offered to pay for the cremation,
I asked about flowers,
Why no flowers?
A white rage should I not get to send them.

No, absolutely not, do not send them . . .
So, I sang to his soul damned as it was.
I opened the window & said – I forgive you.
I'm not sure I do though.
Do I?
Forever, his death, will have been taken into someone's soft
manicured hands.
An eradication, so brutal,
so fast, so fucking breathtakingly efficient.

SO HURT BY ALL OF IT, I THOUGHT DEATH MIGHT BE NICE

Gimmick dice throws a double six.
Clock bites the little hand back.

A Babylonian star cult criticised my curtains.
I've not lined them yet. So?

Ghosts lounge on furniture.
Infuse it with smoke, sneer and snipe.

They are so resentful of the living.
Everything is wasted on us!

Aghast at the art I draw whilst naked.
Inspecting how I iron (badly).

This lot were wash-house girls
before the true cult called.

Each one proclaims each day
how modern life is just so wrong.

Yet when the others aren't looking
they admire cornicing I coated three times,

coo over a black-slate fireplace I cleaned
with toothbrush, wire wool and songs,

exposing silent beauty
for the first time in fifty years;

those ghosts sigh hopefully,
by my record player.

Attentions seekers!
Every last one of them.

I lock the front door,
pad barefoot to bed.

FUCK THAT

Low-souled saints
have formally given notice;
they will no longer be saving dumb-winged dickheads.

There is no more hope for love.
There will be no delusions of decency.
There will be no joy.

No flight is sacrosanct,
there is no click-click
there is no clack-clack.

Fuck hate.
Fuck this life!
Fuck you. Fuck that.

QUEER DATING

It's not hard to figure out who the swan would sleep with just on looks, she is blonde, huge tits, lovely smile, curve to her nose, the long wavy hair of an old Hollywood actress.

The swan doesn't care, she could be any colour, any hair, she could have fifty-seven gold teeth. It is the tits. That's the obsession some days, on others it's more sly, less easy.

The last woman the swan slept with said more than a handful was really just a waste. The swan goes on another queer dating site. Nobody talks. She looks out the window. It is night.

WINDOW

I am watching the wood louse.
It is dead.

Crispy armadillo.
It knows the sloth, yes.

I am watching the wood chip.
Soak it in vinegar.

Those high ceilings
are older than I'll ever be.

I am watching the mountain.
Refusing all distance.

Three horses, two quite mad
and one with a white eye,

the eldest kicks and bites
the littlest one each morning.

Consider cutting its throat.
Consider the blood.

I am watching a stone wall,
it is so easily mossed.

Weather – dread grey!
It arrives in every windowpane

I deliberately
never cleaned them so

they are covered
in hundreds

of smudged handprints
from my three-year-old,

it's where we watch stars,
also for the train

that comes around
a bend

far away
down the valley.

Or in the morning
when a flock of birds

lift and glide as one,
flashing white bellies –

soaring in the light,
fields so green,

still kissed by night!

I DON'T THINK

I can't get well again.
Not this time. Not again.
It's been thirty years.
So many moments unseen by anyone but me.
Hospitals.
Morphine.
Drips.
Collapsed veins.
Every bone hurts for twenty years.
Ears gone.
The tinnitus screaming.
Wake at 3 a.m. and pass out with the pain.
On the floor.
Nobody to find me.
Half a dozen panic attacks a day.
Rigid with fear literally.
Being carried out to an ambulance like a plank of wood.
Asking the psych ward to take me and they say no.
Nobody wants me.
The wanting to jump.
The unbearable!
It's just a decade, or so, that way.
No fucking money means none, a friend asks is that what I
mean . . . it is, aye, no money means none.
No life!
Nasty gaze to how many eyes?
Am I to do more, time?
The sickness. The vomiting. The brain fog. The months not

– 57 –

remembered.

The sadness.

Everything is sticky.

So many kinds of dying.

The agoraphobia.

Stand behind a door panicking for three years.

The walking on roads that feel like huge rolling waves but trying to still act normal.

The demons throwing my body across ceilings for years and returning me to a drenched bed

and expecting me to go Tesco and the dole.

The things how many other's did?

Me in a bathroom after, not meeting my own eyes.

Me not telling.

So much not telling.

Not saying.

Just taking it.

My knuckles just bones.

Child's hands.

Child's feet.

Child's hope.

Child's sorrow.

The kind of hurt that annihilates every future.

Headaches of death.

The bile.

The ambulances.

The bottles of gin. The food stuffed into a mouth to keep a body going that long since lost its sense of any kind of reason to be.

The forcing myself to pick up a hammer.

Knock down walls.

The dust.

The decay.

The judgement.

The hate.

The closed doors.

The fist.

The spit.

The wounds inflicted by ones who smile at others.

The days.

The nights.

The trying. The trying. The trying.

To bring light . . .

I don't know if I can try to get well, again.

Please, God, do I have to do it always by myself?

I can't. Not this time.

ON ANOTHER ONE OF MY WORST YEARS

I write a novel as an epiphany to the universe
on behalf of humanity (no, nobody asked me to
do it please do fuck off)
It's the only thing I can think of to do,
I meet in the place,
of words,
those who are not from here . . . . you see?

NO PERMISSION SLIP REQUIRED

I was not allowed to be a daughter,
or a sister,
or a grandchild,
or a niece,
I was never a fiancée,
nobody called me wife,
I loved women always
though rarely met one who wanted me,
yet still, let me say it like this,
I have lived
I did not need a fucking permission slip.

BENEDICTION

Bottle of whisky every second day on the home shift; sat at the bar 5 p.m. for the daily beers, each night you appeared when the clock struck the hour like a strange kind of cuckoo – holding out stained dollars in your claws, with a toothless smile, limping, all behold the great beaked barfly!

In here there are people who will like you – until 1 a.m. . . . . when the daggers come out, yet until then! It's all love and joie de vivre, everyone likes company for the descent (not me though). Until some time later gills begin to flap, unkempt feet (with thickened yellow toenails) begin to flounder, stagger always meets stoat – no lies, no lies, until all clocks chime, chime, chime – so loud, with sorrow!

One night you look up and everyone – is gone . . . and you pick up your lighter, run it slowly across a wooden bar, metal spokes spray tiny sparks, like when you were wee, remember? Watching the Catherine wheel, the golden light of fireworks in the cold dark night of a Glasgow park.

SPINSTER

It's a long time since I loved anyone.

I will never turn
to another's arms, or scent, or smile,
or kiss, again.

Far too much trauma, Timmy!

Those who deal it out
shrug it off, not seeing (or caring at all)
what they have done . . .

It's been the strangest time.

All trust in me is gone.
There is no girl left in me.
I am only for wolves.

Or, majestic autumn lunes;

I sew my flesh together
with copper,
silently, by a subdued fire.

THEY FOUND SOMETHING IN MY BLOOD

Three weeks ago the high-pitched sound of a
machine declaring my heart dead.

A whee so loud in my ears, it could be heard in space.

Then came the tilt, whenever I tried to walk or
even just sit, tip, tip, tip, tip, tipping.
A giant took my skull.
There always was someone after what was in it.

I lived on a waltzer.
G-force pulling on me all day.

Walking with a cane and even then it's fucking horrific.

At night a wind still warbles its way down the chimney.
I wake at 4 a.m. to dream that the hatch in my attic is open.

A man has clearly got in but I am too jaded to check these days.

I don't care about dying like I used to.
Not as much as I did in my twenties, or thirties, or even last year.

You are gone, I am alone, it's okay, I cry though.
I took down the Christmas tree on 21 December this year, a record,
even for me.

I have given up on the pretence of ritual.
I am just trying to make it out of this year alive,
and praying for a health miracle . . .

WINTER SOLSTICE

My dad drank himself to death this year, bottle of
whisky every second day,
I was sent a photograph of him unconscious with
piles of illegal oxy in front of him.

I have tried.
You wanted to kill me in so many ways:
breakfast tea
to scald bare skin;
honey poured from thighs.
I always used to reach for heat:
a toxic way to die
no dignity,
trauma-bonded.

Many moons on, you hope to see something to pity in me.
Create it where there is only the fatness of skin
left to scorn. You are a fucking idiot.

I hope it repels you
like you do me.
on your way . . .
bemused fud,
that door won't open
back up again.
You are a cheap receptor,
I am illegal opiates.

I've tried to kill myself in so many ways.
Sociopaths, psychopaths, overworking endlessly yet
on this, coldest of winter solstice

as people are failed beyond repair,
I cast a rune, that I will no longer become a ruin,
do not bury me like my people,
long before time
broken by the ignorant
who hope to sell me as insane, okay,
whilst I am still trying to siphon out their poison,
from my shut-down veins.

DO WHAT YOU DO

It is beautiful somewhere but not here.
Very specific linen, fucking hideous!
She likes to keep cultural serial killers in an alibi.
Saviours? Benefactors?
Sorry, what and where?
They are wearers of workers' clothes okay, good joke.
Thicker than shit could ever be.
Manually decayed.
Don't like the wild.
Act as if they do, though.
Capture it in glass baubles.
Shake so, so hard & then screech – this one is faulty!
Do not trust them.
Keep going until you find the few who do not need to
redraw your earthly pistols,
or seek to own – what you hold,
if you don't find them, dear heart, it's okay, just be true . . .
& do what you do, do what you do!

THINGS SAID BY XY CHROMOSOMES

You are a fucking miserable cunt.

The first time I met you, you looked like a French whore.

Your hair is so thick and black and nice.

Get back here!

You shoot well for a girl.

I am warning you.

Women never achieved anything.

Don't underestimate me.

You know most men really hate women?

Slut!

You love it don't you?

You're just a dirty from a children's home.

The door is locked.

Nobody is coming.

Your voice grates.

Your voice makes me feel nauseous.

How long will your depression last cos it is so fucking boring?

I just want to have a nice time.

Lay down.

Do you like the flowers?

If I saw you in the street I'd want to rape you.

Sorry I thought I was going to split up with her but don't make a big deal about it, it was nothing!

It was just fun.

I've never met anyone like you before.

Why don't you kill yourself?

Go on, just jump off a fucking bridge. Go on! Do it!

Marry me.

I'd give you a baby right now.

I want to drag my nails down your cunt.

Have you been whipped before?

If you try and work out where you are I'll rape you in the arse so fucking badly you'll bleed for a week.

I didn't think you'd bruise that badly.

It went too far, I know.

I shouldn't have brought up your childhood rapes when I was fucking you.

I know I did it twice.

I fucking hate you!

No, you weren't unconscious.

Do you speak any other languages? I like German girls. Would you dress up as a Nazi?

Can I eat a bit of your skin? I'd like to fry it with some olive oil.

Do you want me to teach you how to be a sociopath?

You are an angel.

The key to smuggling is you need to not care if you do time.

They'd rape you just to get to me.

If I can't have you nobody will.

Do you like crack?

Nag!

Twisted!

Delusional!

Liar!

Fantasist!

You were born for me. I own you.

No, I'm not ashamed to be seen with you.

I'd like to bite your nipples off.

I'm addicted to you.

I'd kill for you. I'd kill you. Let me suffocate you.

Imagine if I had to say you died during a sex game?

I thought you'd like it. Turn over. Do you want to still be friends?

You don't seem interested in what I'm doing now.

I own your arms. I own your pussy. I'm not jealous of your talent.

You can't cook eggs.

Nothing you have to say will ever mean anything.

Women all bleed on the same day.

You are being watched.

Isn't it terrifying someone could just come to your doorstep and kill you?

I really want to piss on you in silence and shove you out the fucking door.

I killed someone.

I didn't kill anyone.

Yes, the scars were from torture.

I love you. I'd do anything for you. I'm obsessed with you.

I heard your voice when you were not there.

Nobody is coming.

The door is locked.

Marry me.

I've met you in another life before this.

We are together all the time. Even when we are apart I am with you.

It was meant to be.

Do you like to chop vegetables?

Clean that fucking cat litter!

I'll smack you one!

I won't do it again. Open the door – cunt! Get back here or I'll slap you. If my sister wasn't next door I'd batter you right now. You are the one for me. You've broke my heart.

Come home.

POLONIUM-210

I've got the kind of grace,
that people think a Dayton Project
for all their poison . . .

I used to be so grateful –
for anyone even speaking to me
I'd take anything over nothing.

I'd say thank you! Thank you!
Yes, please do give me as much
of your cruelty and hatred as you need.

No, it is no bother!
None at all, please, load it up,
I can take so much, so, so, so much.

Every interaction as a child,
held the blueprint of transaction.
I was designed only to exist

My darling hag years though!
Mean I survived all and more so,
I, with this emitter – return all of it.

Every intact glass vial
I was forced to sip, every cut,
every wrong, every evil –

To those who bequeathed me their wrongs,
I returned them threefold,
they were not mine to carry!

Those low gamma rays
did not belong to me.
Your acts are yours not mine.

You treated me as sub-human.
Never even felt bad about it!
I used to wonder about all that

when I still had hope
that most people were good.
I've long gone beyond that now.

Historically radium-F,
isotope of polonium,
alpha decay – to stable.

PRE-NUPTIAL

If this was a marriage,
of me to me,
I've wanted out,
the whole time;
I wasn't satisfied with how I treated myself for a start,
took me for granted,
worked me to a point of chronic illness,
then blamed my – self,
cheated on myself with those who hurt, humiliated, shamed or
fucked me over,
I was living on my nerves
sought out mediation,
for me, myself and I,
waking up every day – still me,
this mind relentless as time,
seeking the answers to existence before coffee,
every fucking day;
I couldn't divorce myself
no judge would decree it –
until one day I decided to court myself,
go out on a date,
offer myself the kind of service I'd saved solely to impress others,
I cut out the cunts one by one,
bought myself a cauldron and an oar,
set out at night across the sea by moonlight
to read myself poetry . . .
gave myself compliments and realised it was trauma
that did not believe I could do anything,

or that I was worth nothing, at all, it was that, which
had kept me bound . . .
Not me.

WILD WINTER HAG

The wild winter hag
has a bottle
in the shape of a ship;
sunk on ice,
it hangs from her hip,
and this lowest winter sun of the year
won't stop her; there she is, by the shore,
breathing out ice-formations
for the sea
so intricate a gift.

The wild winter hag
has bones
of ancient strata
spalling and arrant cold
in her eyes;
you can see each starlit sky –
from all of time,
when she looks up . . .
all the eons pass –
right in front of you.

INSTEAD OF GOODBYE

You cut me
a clean one
this last time

did you not,
old man?

Split open
like surgery
cleaved . . .

Of all those
who sucked

my bones
clean and spat
it was you first,

you last.

BUSY

She's busy. So busy.
So busy. So busy. So busy.
She can see you in sixteen months for a second.
So busy. She's so busy.
So busy. So busy. So busy.

I FORGOT ABOUT LOVE

I forgot about love;
I was in a true dark night of the soul and it didn't allow for the pretence
of light, no;
so, I forgot . . . about the sound of you playing guitar
in other rooms
whilst I did things peacefully;
you bringing me strawberries and champagne on a tray,
when I was in my little homeless accommodation bedsit . . . just
sixteen years old
and pretty for you,
I forgot about being a child helping one of many grans
(the best one) bake a cake,
I forgot about laughing,
I forgot about the way my baby smiled each morning like I was
the sun come to shine,
how I once cried so hard about how frightened I was by everything
and how you held me,
how you knew a part of myself that I never quite caught,
I forgot about packing a sheepskin coat, money, cigarettes, making
sandwiches, packing books,
blankets, waterproofs, a torch, a spoon, a fork, cleansing cloths,
taking them out to a homeless young guy I could see from my window
and I had nothing really,
except for things others had given or I'd found in charity shops,
but I knew exactly how it felt to have nowhere at all to go
and his smile when I stopped to have a wee chat, just a moment, of
saying, I see you
I'm sorry you are hurting, people too are built on love;

I forgot about so much because of all the words said by men and the
hurt,
the actions, the vile incandescence of their hatred,
I forgot about love because of all those years of alone time, and the
mean horrid stuff when I was grown
and thought I would not have had to go through such horror anymore,
how that took me from me and how the ones who could have cared,
by then, did not . . .
and how much I fought . . . too, on my own,
I am telling you I forgot about love, I turned my face the other way,
it had done nothing for me, in the longest time, it had made me
more unsafe, more lonely, more tired,
I'd gone too far down in the descent by then,
free dived all the way down to beyond the challenger deep,
to depths where breath is not possible
and the only creatures there never saw daylight even once,
they are so strange, and some might call them ugly
but down there I'm just like them:
bare skinned and raw with all the pain of humanity popping
out in pustules:
a current pulls me down, ever further, and I am choosing to go there,
so that I can settle a score . . .
a debt left, in me, by the evil of others' misplacement,
I am facing every darkness,
so that, I won't forget . . . anymore, about love –
not even when my heart is so broken,
my soul inimitably weary, not when I am besieged by historical shame
and fear and panic and hate,

– 81 –

when it feels so much of my fucking life was about being used as a vessel,
a deposit for others' hideous treatment,
and I kept trying to turn all that into art and light,
until I could no longer shine.
I forgot about love,
I forgot about love,
I forgot, I forgot, I forgot . . . about love –
yet it did not forget about me.

OSSIFICATION

I have to go;
I'm ten –
only one of us can die.

I pass through a needle in a ship.
Sail it right
through the universe . . .

Uncut hatred.
It is tattooed on my lassie bones.
New enamel, grows over old.

BADGER

Dearest darling badger moon –

I am tethered to you . . . .
by particles
                of

  me.

ABSTRACT ART

Genetic derangement!

To you I was the most abstract art:
mouth for eyes,
a skyscraper nose;

You stood in a gallery
before me – so, so drunk and swayed,
you peered before blacking out . . .

Where my heart once was,
what's that?

It's a black star.
It's twelve horses breathing fire.
It's a drum so loud

it pounds from my atriums

across the universe –
an inescapable . . . rhythm.

CLEAN BONES

I was an idiot.
I'd see the butcher's hook,
think it a silver hoop.

A clutch of delusion
dabbed behind each ear,
I prayed for love . . .

or even that one person
on earth
might know me.

FUCK IT

He never once put his coat on a hook
not in my home you see –
his entire life was an elaborate act of leaving,
I still protected him from the truth
of my trauma and all the hows in which it got there
and what it did there,
how it riddled me like a cancer
eating chunks of bone,
brain, marrow, lungs, yet only finally
with this last bequeath from him . . .
any even vague
last semblance
of
hope.

MENTAL CONTROL LABORATORY

The average person has around four-thousand thoughts per day. Clearly they are under achieving. The word 'obsess' has a military background, all the way from the 1500s, to obsess a city was to surround but not yet control it. Then the possidere would conquer. A high place phenomenon is a fear of throwing oneself somewhere, anywhere, everywhere high. Ego syntonic is thoughts that might be in line with our drives but they can make us unhappy and we do not question why we have them. Intrusive thoughts that make up obsessions are ego dystonic, Churchill (imperialist cunt, I know) couldn't travel by ship or stand by an approaching train, or balconies, even when he was not suicidal, he couldn't shake those thoughts. Daniel Wegner ran the Mental Control Laboratory before he died of motor neurone disease, he was a white bear guy who showed why forbidden love offers the most thrills, the rebound effect of thought suppression means it will just come back more intense later, I have had millions of intrusive thoughts I think, they are still horrid, I hate them, that's the OCD of it rather than just letting it pass, I am trying though, to know that it is what it is, as often as I can.

STRUGGLING

I am struggling to live in this body.

I am struggling to live on this earth,

I am struggling to live with all the humans.

I am struggling to live with this mind.

I am struggling to live without a family (except my son).

I am struggling to always know I am a good mum (I am the best).

I am struggling to know I can do this (I can't).

I am struggling to live with men (I don't).

I am struggling to live with abusive ex partners.

I am struggling to live with constant daily pain for decades.

I am struggling to live.

I am struggling to live with my history.

I am struggling to live with the reality of putting my memoir out.

I am struggling to live with the truth of my own narrative.

I am struggling to live.

I am struggling to live with so much unfairness.

I am struggling to live with the outcome of long-term gaslighting.

I am struggling to live with the responsibility of light.

I am struggling to live in this pandemic.

I am struggling to live with awareness of wars' destruction.

I am struggling to live with helplessness.

I am struggling to live with fury.

I am struggling to live with the ignorance of others being used as an
excuse to ruin lives.

I am struggling to live in a world where so many people are
profitably mind blind.

I am struggling to live without blowing up my social work files.

I am struggling to live when those who knew me longest and who I loved most have died.

I am struggling to live with my desire to make this world better.

I am struggling to live with what man is doing to the earth when she is so utterly spectacular.

I am struggling to live with injustice.

I am struggling to live with sorrow.

I am struggling to live with casual and cultivated cruelty.

I am struggling to live with worry.

I am struggling to live with reality.

I am struggling to live with existence.

I am struggling to live with death.

I am struggling to live with want.

I am struggling to live with wanting to do so much more to help but feeling utterly fucking useless.

I am struggling to live with heightened empathy.

I am struggling to live with standing up for myself and then being accused of being things I'm not.

I am struggling to live with my broken heart which refuses to not see love.

I am struggling to live with food.

I am struggling to live with the incandescent sharpness of sight.

I am struggling to live with time.

I am struggling to live with history.

I am struggling to live with demons doing ballroom at the dancehall.

I am struggling to live.

I am struggling.

I am.

HOME

It's a thing I heard said once.
It's a rumour.
Some kind of death spell.
It's a nimbie-pimbie-knock-knock!
It's a ne'er do well.
It's a back doorstep to smoke on and drink early morning tea.
It's creepy, it is diseased.
It's a myth-moth!
It's fliff-floff.
It's a tragic trail.
It's a broken tail.
It's a mistaken sign.
It's claw marks in the cupboard.
It's a sourceless bang.
It's a little shrink.
It is a record that goes pfft pfft pfft!
It's over the sea.
It's got no door.
Every window is an old soul.
It's a doom-tide.
It's a kind hymn.
It's not mine but if it was I'd give it back.
It's unholy.
It's a nice dream though,
you'd like it.

I MISS YOU KNOWING ME AND BEING ABLE TO HOLD YOU

I'm holding my hands out to air:
arms in a Y
that is never a letter
I can make peace with, instead I circle it in incense with an O;
you were so beautiful to me
in your weakest, worst, most shameful moments – where others misunderstood
where they only saw a body dying-on-show
as it . . . goes;
I saw you without waiver
knew that you were a sacred heart
remembered your strong and fuckable and incandescent with shine;
I didn't care if they didn't know it
you still had that even if they couldn't see,
it was so hard to watch you go like that before me
and to try to make you smile and feel loved and still seen for you . . .
it's all I could do
and I know what it is to feel so ugly, I do,
to have your body fail you over and over whilst it tries to keep you alive
a little more
and to have to make peace with the raging-visibility of your own fucking struggle,
I will never be a swan
in the way I as a little girl so badly hoped to one day be,
to find my neck elongated
feathers strong,
nope, I hobble in the kitchen when the bones hurt too much

and every mark laid on me shows
every pain, every psychopath I survived
took their ounce of beauty
it's there in how ill I've been for thirty years now
and there's nothing in the way I wear my fat that is fashionable
although I admire those that do;
every time someone wanted to take another bit of that girl I was
and the woman I hoped I would be,
it's there, and it's often all that those that don't know me . . . see,
I'm not hipster fucking marketable
and I hate hipsters
although I like looking at some of them
and when I am exhausted which is nearly always I am all hag and no
gentle lines to soften
the viewer's judgement
I am what I am
someone who has done thirty years ill
and forty-four surviving more than I ever should really but I did it
anyway
because that's the kind of savage bitch I am, still with this open fucking
heart that just won't close!
Neither fashionably fat, nor untetherably pretty
I don't look fuckable when selling my books which I don't actually sell
cos I can't turn up most of the time,
I just write them
and I am still holding my hands out to the air . . . . just as wide as I can
tears ever pouring like a waterfall of every thing I never lost

but today I cry like this for one hurt only,
because you knew me
and I fucking loved you, I loved you so, so, so, so . . .
and I don't know why so many of my people are gone when I had so few
to start with,
but in my ugliest recorded minutes
when the eyes on me are not soft with any kindness I know
I will remember how you loved me, how you loved me, so.

HOMICIDAL MOTIVATIONS

The papers are owned by posh pricks
peddling propaganda from the edge ay a cliff . . .
why do they want tae terrorise old people?
What did the grannies who cannae even afford
lemon curd fae Lidl anymair, ivvir do tae them?
Or the disabled? Or the poor? Or children stuck on boats?
Or the dead ones who lay face down on the shore?
What about ma neighbour who went quietly?
That seems tae be exactly what they like to terrorise!
Such loud declarations they make aw day though!
Constant blaring make it hard to avoid their diligence.
Is it just . . . tae destroy all of fucking humanity?
A privileged kind ay – sport?
Just a wee game, ay?

IN ANOTHER COUNTRY

My father's body is burned
without last rites,
no ceremony,
no service,
no family,
no obituary,
no flowers.

I have no choice in any of it.
He's dead.
So they say.

THE BOQUET

Who will love me?

It's a bold no!
It's a yo-yo.
It's a no-go zone with territorial hypoxia.

Don't ask the exes!
The gifts they bore: delusion, antipatico, psychopathery, narcissi,
revile, invective, obloquy.

I arrange flowers for my own funeral.
It will fall on a Wednesday.

Who will love me?

Not those who try to inseminate my light with their poison.
Stab each heart vein, each Venus cava (superior and inferior) with
their own unique virus.
How deleterious!

If I die they don't die.

They walk taller after taking –
what they can of who I am.

Nocents: sicken body, mind and soul.

I arrange flowers for my own funeral.
In a window where the sun shines, it is beautiful.

I shall say, when delivering
my own report to the god source,
life failed in most, nearly all, elements of care.

I will say it as politely as that.
Manners maketh the me-moth.

I doubt she would disagree.

I arrange flowers for my own funeral.
It is radiant.

Who will love me?

I know who did and I'm more grateful than a dying minaret.
Each act of kindness!

Those who unravel laughter and bring such light!
Not those who scream that they are normal – whilst pustules of
their own brain sickness (the one they refuse to ever see) made
me so ill.

I carry what they can't
& they question if I am blessed?

I arrange flowers for my own funeral.
This poem is the first boquet . . .

such long stems,
well-thorned, flowers red.

LET'S BANG ON ABOUT THE MOON

Poets and the fucking moon.
Fucking poets.
Fucking moons.
Dinnae get me started!

What if the moo–OOOn was a mushroo–ooom?
What if it wiz a mUSh moon?

What if you were a cunt?
What if you were an absolute fUCKing cUnT?
Poets and the fucking moon?
Poets being fucking cunts!

Fuck poets.
Fuck the moon.

LUMINARY

Coral obituaries, I've earned success
waiting tables for Cuban fighters.

Obviously –
I am superb!

I was only in it for the words.
I did not like baseless performers, no!

Sharp-elbowed.
Ominous side-eye.

People weren't often who they said they were.
I missed who they were not!

MORTAR

I am in so much pain right now
for the first time in years I'd take the comfort of flesh
skin to skin, bones that ache, by my bones that ache,
the frenetic grinding down
on the mortar of minutes,
whittling back all the fucking noise of life,
hands gripping, feet pushing,
tongues seeking, hope dying, not caring,
just wanting, a person to fuck it all away with in fury,
holding on to them like they were the only person on earth to hold onto,
then to sleep . . .
knowing there is someone to reach for in the dark,
& to sometimes wake,
in the slow quiet,
of a world not yet risen,
to find I am still being reached for,
somewhere to turn,
soft, raw, uncontainable,
sway, from the blade,
of the knife.

BEFORE HE DIES

He looks like a little boy:
legs I'd never seen before
so curiously hairless,
hallowed cheeks.
She sent me photographs
on the day he died,
her gleeful goodbye,
before his body is burnt,
no obituary, no funeral
no last rites, no will
(she said he lied about me being in it)
So, I decided to give you the only thing I could . . .
forgiveness,
for all you'd put me through
from birth to death;
I took an oath to grant you absolution,
it was all you actually needed
to ascend.

THE TAKER

When the person who only knew how to take
continues to leech your soul,
even in absence
sow a row of red tulips
into the wounds where your heart needs to heal.

SHE PLAYED THE TROMBONE, YOU KNOW

I mostly wake alone;
this world has no trinkets,
I don't care,
I have plants to water,
books to order,
I have things to read, to re-read, to never read, to definitely
never read, to one day read,
stars scatter their vastness;
I once recited poetry to the pharaoh's echo
in the King's Pyramid, Egypt,
slept many nights in Shakespeare and Company in Paris;
I cried at Frank Black,
Patti Smith,
I danced all night in wee grunge clubs,
slept once on a very large French kitchen table,
still quite drunk,
it was after the fireworks and the dancing in the village with
everyone,
I went to the lake in the early mist
and asked my god
not to spare me pain;
I knew I could carry it in copper milk pails,
so I too could still sip – whilst sorrowed
on the nectar of existence;
I met love
and held it,
and I never, ever, ever forgot
the ones who went with my loyalty

in this life,
or the next place,
I laid out my long, long neck each night,
a tiny trumpet in each ear
blares out –
this, this, this, this, this!

TRIFFID

I used to glow at night as I slept,
like a triffid
from the future
that did not yet know
how-to-not radiate,
long-toothed
sabre narcissists
spied my shallow breaths,
saw my sparkle,
saw my circles of forget,
drank deeper
than vampires –
devoid of humanity,
it was just a husk each of them left . . .
despite the collateral damage
(not fucking insubstantial)
I survived all deaths,
I got up to make hot tea
after each assassination attempt,
missing a liver,
missing a leg,
I held a mirror up to malevolence
to find poison
on its manky breath;
I took the suns
from my eyes,
placed them back up in the sky,
I glowed – even fucking brighter then,

I still had uncut love to give,
refused to slit my own soul into slivers,
for others' fucked up shit,
my heart is
far more punk than flesh,
it belongs to me, not life, or death,
nor any of the malignant I hereby choose – to forget.

DEAD AT THE HELM

A hulking grey ship
glides by the harbour
in a Newhaven haar.

Dead at the helm,
drag slowed by avoirdupois
souls sail – towards a reckoning.

SINGING NINA SIMONE TO THE ECHO

A court psychologist
solemnly informed me my life
was so saturated in abuse
that I'd never recover
I'd suffer
and be unwell
until I die.

I wondered who told her that?
She's clearly never heard me sing old Nina Simone songs in a
stairwell at 6 a.m.

ONE DAY

When the butcher is no longer strong,
when the day is turning to a purple dusk,
when the feeling of safety has long since returned,
when I know the fireflies,
when there has been a porch to sweep for decades,
when I think of the young woman
with a whole world
of fear, pain, to traverse,
how she did it,
quietly and unseen
I will celebrate her tenacity, that put me, on the way, to home.

I'VE MADE HOUSES PERFECT

I've made houses perfect
then sat in them gazing at the view like a burglar in someone else's life
for a minute before the real people arrive
come to the door with actual money to claim it and they do,
I made this one for me and this one for you,
I want the one that is truly for my son, for cats we don't have to let go
to hold our future,
I took all I had in me, tenacity, claw, tooth, blood, spit, fury, exhaustion,
such tiredness,
the filth under my fingernails,
achy days,
dirty clothed and unwashed hair,
stress and a worry of death,
working on the top rung of the ladder alone
freezing my fingertips
in Frida's chapel,
panicking on the roof in winter but still getting it all done and more,
I won't do it for another again,
they took far more than they had the right to,
a four letter word is sacred to me even more now than it ever was:
H.O.M.E.

HOPE

I hope when I die
nearly all the memories my mind plays in those moments
after death, or whilst dying,
are of you . . .
because you were the best thing that ever happened to me,
and to get a chance
in passing,
to see you in all of those moments
before leaving this existence,
will bring me a final memory of true gratitude
and joy.

THANK YOU

To the poetry
that found me
at seven years old
in a caravan park;
cold stones in my pockets
I was cursed to carry.

You waited on a blank page
for my ink to meet you;
in that second
a gift was given
that I have never let go,
yet even as a child . . .

I didn't ever try to hold you,
it would be
like trying to cup
a hummingbird in your hands
and thinking it would still
be able to sing its song.

I just wanted to say,
thank you,
through every situation,
you were there for me,
no matter what was going on,
never judging . . .

In return you never tried –
to hold me,
you taught me instead
that to truly sing . . .
means to let go of all notes
just like a soul – finally free to soar.

ACKNOWLEDGEMENTS

Thank you to all who read my poetry and resonate, who write to me; thank you to Edward Crossan who has kept me company in the edits of all these collections, and whose eye is sharp and more; thank you to everyone at Polygon who makes beautiful books for me, it is so appreciated; to the booksellers who keep this entire pivot turning; thank you to the poets who left breadcrumbs for all of us to find in the forest; for the kind ones; for the feral; for those who have given me love and allowed me to know what it is to have awe for another's soul; for those who know how to hear and have gone out to bring home silence; to the truth tellers and the dignified; to the furious; to those who do not stop walking for others as much as themselves; thank you to the moon, I am sorry I drag you through this on every collection and most novels too; however, you must hang there each night, far above dreaming poets, utterly beguiling.